Superstars
of the
CHICAGO
BEARS

by Matt Scheff

amicus
high interes

Amicus High Interest is published by Amicus
P.O. Box 1329, Mankato, MN 56002
www.amicuspublishing.us

Library of Congress Cataloging-in-Publication Data
Scheff, Matt.
  Superstars of the Chicago Bears / Matt Scheff.
     pages cm. -- (Pro sports superstars)
  Includes index.
  ISBN 978-1-60753-522-5 (hardcover) -- ISBN 978-1-60753-552-2 (eBook)
  1. Chicago Bears (Football team)--History--Juvenile literature. 2. Football
players--United States--Biography--Juvenile literature. I. Title.
  GV956.C5S34 2014
  796.332'640977311--dc23
                            2013006830

Photo Credits: John Swart/AP Images, cover; Tom DiPace/AP Images, 2, 15;
Greg Trott/AP Images, 5; AP Images, 6, 13, 16, 22; NFL Photos/AP Images,
9; Pro Football Hall of Fame/AP Images, 11; Frederick Breedon/AP Images,
19; Scott Boehm/AP Images, 20

Produced for Amicus by The Peterson Publishing Company
and Red Line Editorial.

Editor Jenna Gleisner
Designer Becky Daum
Printed in the United States of America
Mankato, MN
July, 2013
PA 1938
10 9 8 7 6 5 4 3 2 1

TABLE OF CONTENTS

MEET THE CHICAGO BEARS

The Chicago Bears were one of the first **NFL** teams. The Bears have won a Super Bowl. They are known for great **defense**. The Bears have had many stars. Here are some of the best.

BRONKO NAGURSKI

Bronko Nagurski was one of the Bears' first stars. He was big and strong. He played **offense** and defense. He helped the Bears win the championship in 1933.

Nagurski helped the Bears win three NFL championships.

MIKE DITKA

Mike Ditka was a **tight end**. Most tight ends at the time just blocked the other team. Ditka did more. He was also great at catching passes. He scored 12 touchdowns in 1961.

Ditka later coached the Bears. He helped the Bears win a Super Bowl.

GALE SAYERS

Gale Sayers was hard to catch. He was fast. He had great moves. Sayers scored six touchdowns in one game in 1965. That is still a record.

DICK BUTKUS

Some call Dick Butkus the best **linebacker** ever. He was smart. He was fast and strong, too. Few runners ever got past him. He retired in 1973.

WALTER PAYTON

Walter Payton had speed and power. He was one of the best **running backs** ever. He was the **MVP** of the NFL in 1977. He helped the Bears win a Super Bowl.

Payton had sweet moves. That is why fans called him "Sweetness."

15

MIKE SINGLETARY

Mike Singletary hit hard. He played middle linebacker. He played great defense. He went to ten **Pro Bowls** in a row. The last one was in 1992.

BRIAN URLACHER

Brian Urlacher was a tackling machine. He joined the Bears in 2000. Right away, he was one of their best players. He won an award for playing great defense in 2005. He had 98 tackles.

Urlacher made more tackles than any other Bears player.

LANCE BRIGGS

Lance Briggs is another star on defense. He is always around the ball. He hits hard and forces fumbles. He has played almost every game since 2003.

The Bears have had many great players. Who will be the next?

TEAM FAST FACTS

Founded: 1919

Other Names: Decatur Staleys (1919-1920), Chicago Staleys (1921)

Nicknames: The Monsters of the Midway, Da Bears

Home Stadium: Soldier Field (Chicago, Illinois)

Super Bowl Titles: 1 (1985)

NFL Championships: 9 (1921, 1932, 1933, 1940, 1941, 1943, 1946, 1963, and 1985)

Hall of Fame Players: 27, including Bronko Nagurski, Mike Ditka, Gale Sayers, Dick Butkus, Walter Payton, and Mike Singletary

WORDS TO KNOW

defense – the group of players that tries to stop the other team from scoring

linebacker – a player whose main job is to tackle the other team so they cannot score

MVP – Most Valuable Player; an honor given to the best player each season

NFL – National Football League; the league pro football players play in

offense – the group of players that tries to score

Pro Bowl – the NFL's all-star game

running back – a player whose main job is running with the ball.

tight end – a player whose main jobs are to catch passes and block

LEARN MORE

Books
Frisch, Aaron. *Chicago Bears*. Mankato, MN: Creative Education, 2011.

LeBoutillier, Nate. *The Story of the Chicago Bears*. Mankato, MN: Creative, 2010.

Web Sites
Chicago Bears—Official Site
http://www.chicagobears.com
Watch video clips and view photos of the Chicago Bears.

NFL.com
http://nfl.com
Check out pictures and your favorite football players' stats.

NFL Rush
http://www.nflrush.com
Play games and learn how to be a part of NFL PLAY 60.

INDEX